EASTBOURN

Volume 1

A Portrait in Old Picture Postcards

by

John Wilton and John Smith

Foreword

by

Penny Johnson

S.B. Publications
1990

FOREWORD

Little did we at the Towner Art Gallery and Local History Museum realise that the exhibition of postcards organised in 1988 would inspire this publication. The exhibition was short lived but now some of those images collected in this booklet can be viewed permanently at leisure.

Eastbourne became a popular resort in the late 19th century following the establishment of the railway in 1849. Much of the grand architecture which gives Eastbourne its character today was built during this period. Such architecture combined with the sea views and carpet gardens set against the splendid backdrop of the South Downs provided ample scope for the photographer to capture appealing images of Eastbourne for picture postcards.

Postcards nowadays are avidly collected. They give an invaluable insight into the social history of the time. Through the messages and greetings we can learn about the social mores and sentiments of the period, while the images reveal how the topography of a place changes or develops over the years. We content ourselves in the discovery that Eastbourne's sea-front has little changed compared with its centre and the publication of a booklet such as this enriches our appreciation of Eastbourne's history.

Penelope Johnson
Curator
March 1990

INTRODUCTION

The first pictures on postcards in this country were published in 1894. These early picture cards were known as 'Court Cards', smaller in size than the standard cards of today, and sharing the space of one side with the correspondence. In 1902, the standard size was introduced and new Post Office regulations permitted one side of the postcard to be used for the illustration, and the reverse side for the correspondence and the address.

During the early years of this century, millions of postcards were posted annually, encouraged by the cheap ½d postage rate and the vast output and choice of postcards published, depicting every subject imaginable. This era was known as the 'Golden Age of Postcards'.

Postcard collecting became a national craze and almost every household could boast of an album of cards for visitors to see and admire. The usage and collection of postcards remained very popular until the end of World War I, after which it went into a gradual decline, caused mainly by a rise in postage rates and the increased use of the telephone. Many fine collections were to lie dormant for many years and it is only during the last ten years that they have been rediscovered and today postcard collecting is as popular as ever.

Topographical cards are the most sought after by today's collectors. Local cards are no exception and are in great demand, especially the better photographic examples and rare specimens depicting railways or historic events.

During the 'Golden Age' there were numerous postcard publishers. These included the national firms of Raphael Tuck, Valentine's, Judge's and Frith's, and local publishers such as Carter & Co. of 17 Terminus Road, J. Pulsford, and L. A. J. Vinall at the Meads Library; all combining to leave a comprehensive record of life in the town during the first twenty years of this century.

The name Eastbourne means eastern stream, derived from the Old English word burna (stream). This particular stream rises near St. Mary's Church, Old Town and still flows today. In Saxon times a small settlement was established close to the stream. The Domesday Book records the village as Burne, by the thirteenth century it was known as Estburn, and over the centuries the name changed to East Burn and eventually to Eastbourne.

In the nineteenth century, two great landowners, the Cavendish (Dukes of Devonshire) and Gilbert families were responsible for the creation, planning and development of the elegant town that we see today. The original master-plan was devised by the 7th Duke of Devonshire, his architect Henry Currey, George Ambrose Wallis (the Duke's agent and later the first mayor), and by Carew Davies Gilbert and his surveyor Nicholas Whitely.

INTRODUCTION (continued)

Another significant factor in the development of Eastbourne as a popular seaside resort was the construction of the London, Brighton and South Coast Railway; the first locomotive arriving at Eastbourne Railway Station in 1849. Gradually, over the next twenty years, more and more people came to the town, and by 1870 the population had doubled and visitors were arriving in their thousands. Eastbourne became known as the "Empress of Watering Places" as a result of its excellent climate and patronage of the aristocracy.

Eastbourne, like many other towns, has changed greatly over the last hundred years and is, of course, still changing. The purpose of this book is to show these changes illustrated by old picture postcards, which are now realised to provide an invaluable record for the local historian. The book has been designed to follow two nostalgic tours of the town. The first tour commencing at Holywell and then travelling in a north-easterly direction along the sea-front to the Redoubt. The second tour starts at Upper Duke's Drive and covers an inland route down into Meads and then into the town centre, by way of Seaside, Old Town, Ocklynge and Hampden Park. Finally, the tour ends by returning to Beachy Head and the old Belle Tout Lighthouse.

A second volume is planned in the near future to feature further views of the town, more of the town's social history, with views of Willingdon, Polegate, and the surrounding villages of Eastdean, Jevington, Hankham, Stone Cross, Westham, Pevensey and Pevensey Bay.

We hope that this book will bring back many happy memories to readers who remember Eastbourne as it used to be, will show the younger generation how the town has changed, and give as much pleasure to readers as we have had in selecting these postcards, visiting the locations, talking to local residents and finally writing this book.

John Wilton and John Smith
Eastbourne
February 1990

THE SEAL AND COAT OF ARMS OF THE BOROUGH

The Arms are illustrated on a postcard published by Stoddart & Co. of Halifax in their 'Ja-Ja' heraldic series, which covered almost every city and town in the British Isles.

In 1859, after the inauguration of the local board, it was thought that there should be an official seal. The seal was designed by the well-known Sussex antiguary, Mark Antony Lower. In 1883, the town was given Borough status and the seal retained. The seal was not officially sanctioned and was later withdrawn by Mr. William George Phelps.

In 1928, the College of Arms issued Letters Patent assigning Arms to the County Borough of Eastbourne. The Shield itself is the Arms of the Baronial House of Badlesmere who held the Lordship of Eastbourne in the 13th and 14th centuries. The two stags' horns are from the Cavendish Arms (Duke of Devonshire) and the rose is from the Gilbert Arms. The sea horse is emblematical of the coastal position of Eastbourne. The Latin motto means 'We strive for better things'.

MELIORA SEQVIMUR

EASTBOURNE.

1

Eastbourne from Foot of Beachy Head.

EASTBOURNE FROM THE FOOT OF BEACHY HEAD, p.u. 1928

The view is similar today, though two new buildings have recently appeared. The children's convalescent home, seen on the left, has been replaced by Dolphin Court flats built in 1965 and the 18-storey South Cliff Towers now dominates the skyline. At the foot of the hill are buildings which comprise St. Bede's Preparatory School. St. Bede's was founded in 1895 and now has over 500 pupils.

HOLYWELL AND PINNACLE POINT, p.u. 1921

The path leads down the cliff to Holywell hamlet. Pinnacle Point Rock is in the foreground on the right of the path.

Holywell Eastbourne. 546.

Holywell Retreat, Eastbourne

HOLYWELL RETREAT, p.u. 1908

Holywell is not actually visible. In reality it is obscured by the ridge at the back of the Gore Chalk Pit. The hamlet was situated below what is now St. Bede's School. There is still an access road which leads down past the 'Sugar Loaf', or Pinnacle Point, to what is now a pumping station for the Eastbourne Waterworks Company. There were fishermen's cottages and lime kilns, all of which have disappeared. Chalk quarrying was big business during the early 19th century. The chalk was mostly transported by sea.

Beachy Head and Holywell, Eastbourne.

THE ITALIAN GARDENS AT HOLYWELL, c. 1930

In 1922 the then derelict Gore Chalk Pit was converted into Holywell Italian gardens, which are now a popular spot at the end of the promenade. Even in the driest of summers, water trickles out from the base of the cliffs and clearly this has had some connection with the name 'Holy Well' long ago. Visible on the promenade are chalets let annually by the Borough of Eastbourne. Chalet No. 2 was used in early 1935 by King George V and Queen Mary.

ST. LUKE'S CONVALESCENT HOSPITAL, p.u. 1907
St. Luke's Children's Hospital was opened by the Prince of Wales in 1891 while he was staying
at Compton Place with Princess Alexandra. The hospital has now been replaced by Dolphin Court,
a block of flats opened in 1965.

ALL SAINTS CONVALESCENT HOME, p.u. 1907

In 1867, a nun, Mother Harriett, who during the 1850s had founded a Community known as the All Saints Sisters of the Poor, moved from London to Eastbourne. The Reverend Mother acquired an establishment known as Compton House near St. Saviour's Church in South Street, where 30 convalescent patients were cared for. When Compton House became inadequate to meet the demands upon the community, funds were raised and a site for a new hospital was secured in Meads. The foundation stone was laid in July 1867 by Lady Fanny Howard, a sister of the Duke of Devonshire. On July 19th, 1869, the completed building was blessed and declared open by Dr. Samuel Wilberforce, Lord Bishop of Winchester. In 1958, the hospital was closed and the last of the sisters left Eastbourne.

In 1959, the Ministry of Health purchased All Saints and it is now used by the area Health Authority as a geriatric hospital.

EASTBOURNE. — *Western Parade.* — L.

KING EDWARD'S PARADE, p.u. 1910
The Prince of Wales, later Edward VII opened the extended Western Parade in June 1883.
Chatsworth Court, now used as flats, overlooks the Parade.

3 King Edward Parade and Wish Tower, Eastbourne.

KING EDWARD'S PARADE, p.u. 1936

In 1873 the grounds surrounding the Wish Tower were described as "an occasional potato field". The Local Board spent some £400 laying new gardens, and over the years these pleasant gardens and lawns have always been well maintained by Eastbourne Corporation. On the left of the picture is a wing of the Grand Hotel and beyond it, the Landsdowne Hotel. On the right, the statue of the 8th Duke of Devonshire can be seen on the Western Lawns.

UNVEILING THE STATUE OF THE 8th DUKE OF DEVONSHIRE, 1910

At 1 p.m. on Monday, October 24th, 1910, the Duke of Norfolk unveiled the statue of Spencer Compton, 8th Duke of Devonshire. The statue, sculpted by Mr. Alfred Drury, is sited on the Western Lawns immediately opposite the Grand Hotel. The photograph, taken by a "Gazette" photographer, captures the moment of unveiling when part of the covering, which still clung to the bronze figure, was removed with the assistance of two men. After the ceremony, there was a luncheon at the Grand Hotel. Those present included the Duke of Devonshire, the Duke of Norfolk and Lord Willingdon.

THE GRAND HOTEL, p.u. 1908

The building of the Grand Hotel was completed in 1877. The architect was Robert Knott Blessley who also designed Lushington Road and the Leaf Hall. In 1886 Gowland's Directory describes the hotel's amenities: 'This magnificent hotel facing the sea stands in its own ornamental grounds with tennis lawns at the west end or most fashionable part of Eastbourne. It contains over 200 rooms including a Grand Dining Saloon and Drawing Room, Library, Conservatory, Sitting Rooms with private balconies overlooking the sea and bedrooms en suite, Billiard and Snooker Rooms'. From 1925 until the beginning of the Second World War, the BBC broadcast the Palm Court orchestra every Sunday from the Great Hall in the hotel.

46461. EASTBOURNE: CHURCH PARADE.

CHURCH PARADE ON THE WESTERN LAWNS, c. 1915

At the turn of the century, large numbers of the "well-to-do" would take a leisurely walk on the Western Lawns. Dressed in their finery, they demonstrated their position in society and also, perhaps, the fact that they had been to Morning Service and had a cook at home to prepare luncheon. Peter Pugh, in his book "Grand Hotel", notes: "Western Lawns on Sunday Morning - this was the place to find a wife or husband".

ON THE SANDS, p.u. 1914
In the foreground, children paddle or play with their model boats. Behind them, bathing-machines
stand facing the sea. The correspondent writes: "don't you wish you were by the seaside?".

THE WISH TOWER, p.u. 1910

In 1804, the government decided to build fixed defences between Dover and Beachy Head. They were similar to a defensive tower built by the French at Mortella Point in Corsica. Martello comes from the word "mortella". The Wish Tower is an excellent example of this type of defensive structure and is now a museum. The name Wish is a corruption of Wash, a stream that once flowed here. The Channel Fleet is seen in the background.

14

Wish Tower, Eastbourne

THE WISH TOWER, p.u. 1912

The Victorians enjoyed their stroll along the promenade and sitting on the slopes of the Wish
Tower lawns. Little has changed, but one must wonder if they would have approved of the BBC
Radio One Roadshow which now annually draws large crowds to these slopes.

GRAND PARADE, p.u. 1905

Apart from the people's dress, the view is very similar today. It was along here in 1848 that James Berry, the Earl of Burlington's surveyor, began to construct a sea-wall made of greensand from the nearby quarry. Bathing-machines, which were horse-drawn, can be seen on the foreshore.

Alexandra Hotel.
Eastbourne.

THE ALEXANDRA HOTEL, GRAND PARADE, p.u. 1904
The exterior of the Alexandra, one of the smaller sea-front hotels, has hardly changed at all.
The restaurant is still on the extreme right of the building and the hotel is still run as a family
business.

35 EASTBOURNE. — *The Baths.* — LL.

THE DEVONSHIRE BATHS, p.u. 1906

The Devonshire Baths were designed in 1872 by G. A. Wallis, the Duke of Devonshire's agent and first mayor of Eastbourne, and built close to the junction of Carlisle Road and Grand Parade. The baths opened on 1st April, 1874 and contained two heated sea-water baths filled through an iron pipe from the nearby beach below the Wish Tower. The larger bath was reserved for gentlemen and the smaller bath reserved for ladies. Family bathing was allowed on Mondays, Wednesdays and Saturdays. The baths closed during the 1960s and have been replaced by the Leisure Pool sited on the Crumbles at Langney. The Alexandra Hotel is shown on the left of the photograph and Carlisle Road in the centre.

THE BURLINGTON HOTEL, p.u. 1935

The Burlington Hotel, which was built in 1851, was the first of several majestic hotels erected on the sea-front. It was named after the 2nd Earl of Burlington, later to become the 7th Duke of Devonshire. At the time of its construction there were only a few houses and a greensand quarry between the Wish Tower and the hotel.

THE CAVENDISH HOTEL, p.u. 1906

The Cavendish Hotel, opened in 1873, is situated in a prominent position on the sea-front overlooking the Bandstand. On 22nd November 1940, a bomb ended up stuck through a panel of the door of the saloon-bar - but it failed to explode. However, the hotel was less fortunate in May 1942, when a 250kg. bomb from a ME 109 fighter devastated the east wing. RAF personnel were billeted in the hotel at the time.

AERIAL VIEW OF EASTBOURNE, c. 1920s

The photograph, taken from an "Avro" aeroplane, shows the sea-front from South Cliff to Burlington Place. In the foreground can be seen the Western Lawns, the Wish Tower and the old Lifeboat house. Also visible (from left to right) are the Grand, Lansdowne and Wish Tower hotels, Wilmington Square, the Oban and Alexandra hotels, the Devonshire Baths and the Commmodore hotel (both awaiting re-development). The area between Lascelles Terrace and Howard Square has been redeveloped and is now the site of the T.G.W.U. Holiday, Recuperation and Conference Centre. The West Rock and Sandhurst hotels and Burlington Place are on the extreme right. Open spaces visible in the town include Jevington Gardens, the Eastbourne College playing fields, Devonshire Park - with its tennis courts, and further inland the Saffrons and Gildredge Park. Compton Place can be seen nestling among the trees and behind the house, the Royal Eastbourne Golf Course and what may be the Summerdown Convalescent Camp.

The Parade and Wish Tower, Eastbourne

LOWER PARADE, p.u. 1929
Except for the style of dress, little has changed. Deck chairs still line the Parade and the more
energetic take healthy walks.

EASTBOURNE. — Lower Parade — LL.

WESTERN BANDSTAND, LOWER PARADE, p.u. 1911

The Western Bandstand or "Bird Cage" was built in 1882 and stood on cast iron stilts adjacent to the Lower Parade. The postcard shows a packed promenade with many people listening to the band. Closer inspection reveals some fascinating detail: notice the group of schoolgirls centre right, and the ladies sitting in their Bath chairs - many holding sunshades - on the top balcony.

THE BEACH, p.u. 1916
There was much more shingle in the early part of this century. Horses were used to pull bathing machines up and down the beach. The sea-front hotels line the Parade on the right, and Beachy Head lies in the background beyond the Wish Tower.

CENTRAL BANDSTAND, EASTBOURNE

THE CENTRAL BANDSTAND, c. 1936

The Western Bandstand was replaced in 1935 by the Central Bandstand. It was built on the site of the earlier "Bird Cage" and provided seating for 3000 people. It remains one of the town's major summer attractions, where holidaymakers and local residents can listen to fine performances from military and civilian bands. On the wall of the promenade facing the bandstand is a memorial plaque to John Wesley Woodward; one of the heroic musicians who went down in the 'Titanic' in April 1912. He is remembered because he played the cello in the Grand Hotel orchestra, the Duke of Devonshire's orchestra, and the Eastbourne municipal orchestra.

Eastbourne's Memorial to the 1,056 Men and Women who fell in the Great War, 1914-1919. As it appeared after the Unveiling on November 10, 1920.

THE WAR MEMORIAL, c. 1920
The War Memorial, which commemorates the 1056 men and women who were killed in the 1914-18 War, stands in Memorial Square at the junction of Cornfield Terrace and Devonshire Place. The Memorial, sculpted by Henry Fehr, was unveiled on 10th November 1920.

DEVONSHIRE PLACE, c. 1950

Looking up Devonshire Place towards the sea-front and the statue of the 7th Duke of Devonshire. The War Memorial, in the centre foreground, stands at the junction of five roads: Trinity Trees on the left; Bolton Road and Cornfield Road left and right foreground; and South Street and Cornfield Terrace on the right.

Devonshire Place, Eastbourne

THE STATUE OF THE 7th DUKE OF DEVONSHIRE, c. 1906
The statue of the 7th Duke of Devonshire, sculpted by Mr. Goscombe John, is situated on Grand
Parade at the end of Devonshire Place. The Duke died in 1891 and his statue was erected some
ten years after his death. William Cavendish, 2nd Earl of Burlington and the 7th Duke of Devonshire,
was the principal founder of modern Eastbourne.

32 EASTBOURNE. — The Pier from the Parade. — LL.

BOATS AND BOATMEN, p.u. 1910

The 1897 edition of the town guide "Empress of Watering Places" states that "numerous boats throng the beach from the Redoubt to the Wish Tower and the class of boats ranges from the "Skylark" - an excursion boat, to sailing and rowing boats of all sizes. Without exaggeration, too, it may be stated that the fishermen of Eastbourne are of a superior class, being very civil and obliging, and rowdyism, such as is associated with many seaside boatmen, is unknown".

Royal Sovereign Lightship off Eastbourne

THE ROYAL SOVEREIGN LIGHTSHIP, c. 1910

As the English Channel narrows into the Strait of Dover, numerous hidden shoals and sandbanks lie off the Sussex and Kent coast offering serious hazards to shipping. In the 18th and 19th centuries wooden light-vessels were moored to mark these dangers, but they often dragged their anchors and were unreliable.

In 1875, Trinity House established the Royal Sovereign lightship to mark the Royal Sovereign Shoal, seven miles off Eastbourne. Larger vessels were required to keep a course to the south of the lightship.

In 1966, Sir William Halcrow and Partners were commissioned by Trinity House to investigate the feasability of a light tower structure, and the same year a tender was accepted by Christiani and Nielsen for a concrete structure with a steel tower. The base and tower were constructed at Newhaven commencing in 1967 and finally positioned after many delays in 1971. The new light tower is 159 feet high with the light visible for 28 miles.

Eastbourne—Carpet Gardens.

5675. R. Fishwicke

THE CARPET GARDENS, p.u. 1922
The famous gardens are beautifully kept. They are sited opposite the Burlington Hotel and are
still a glorious site today. Notice the splendid open-topped 'bus on the left.

Eastbourne.   The Pier.

EASTBOURNE PIER, p.u. 1904

Eastbourne Pier was designed by Eugenius Birch, a famous pier designer of the 19th century. Construction of the pier began in 1866, but it was not completed until 1870-71. In January 1877 disaster struck and the shoreward end was destroyed in a great storm. When rebuilt, the pier was on a slightly higher level.

EASTBOURNE PIER, p.u. 1925

This later view of the pier shows the alterations made to the pier entrance and the addition of ornate towers. At the end of the pier were the Pier Pavilion Theatre, sadly destroyed by fire in 1970, and the ballroom, now occupied by an amusement arcade.

Bandstand
and Pier
Pavilion,
Eastbourne

THE PIER PAVILION THEATRE, p.u. 1908
The Pier Pavilion Theatre presented numerous plays which attracted large audiences. During
the Edwardian era, ticket prices ranged from 6d to 2/-, and those from 9d upwards could be
reserved in advance at the pier gates or by telephone (Eastbourne 574). In more recent years,
and before the theatre's destruction, the most famous performer, who appeared regularly, was
Sandy Powell known as 'Mr. Eastbourne'.

THE PIER PAVILION THEATRE, 1909

A publicity postcard illustrating members of Taylor Platt and Trevor Lowe's Company who performed "You Never Can Tell", a farcical comedy in four acts by Bernard Shaw. Advertised as the wittiest play of its time, it had run for four successful seasons at the Court and Savoy Theatres, London, and had returned to Eastbourne for its third season in 1909. Commencing on Monday, 13th July, performances ran for six nights starting at 8 p.m. (matinees on Wednesday and Saturday at 3 p.m.).

39 EASTBOURNE. — "Brighton Queen" leaving Eastbourne. — LL.

P.S. "BRIGHTON QUEEN" LEAVING EASTBOURNE PIER, p.u. 1908

During the summer months, trips from the end of the pier were always popular. Pleasure-steamers sailed to the Royal Sovereign lightship, Brighton, Hastings, and as far as Shanklin on the Isle of Wight. Even up to the early 1950s, a paddle-steamer called occasionally at the pier. The paddle-steamer *Brighton Queen* was the best-loved of all Sussex steamers. She was built in 1897 by the Clydebank Shipping and Engineering Company for the Brighton, Worthing and South Coast Steamboat Company: 240 ft. in length, 553 gross tonnage, with a maximum speed of 20 knots. The *Brighton Queen* made numerous cross-channel excursions but sadly had a relatively short life. She was requisitioned by the Admiralty in September 1914, and on the night of the 5th October, 1915, during mine-sweeping duties off the Belgian coast, she struck a mine and sank.

CHANNEL FLEET, EASTBOURNE /// S. C. & Co. 89

CHANNEL FLEET OFF EASTBOURNE PIER, 1914
A rare postcard photographed on 6th July 1914, showing part of the Channel Fleet anchored on the horizon. P. & A. Campbell's paddle-steamer *Ravenswood* can be seen approaching Eastbourne Pier, along with a wide variety of craft including a number of naval steam picket boats.

THE UNVEILING OF THE ROYAL SUSSEX REGIMENT MEMORIAL, 1906
On Wednesday, 7th February 1906, the Duke of Norfolk, Lord Lieutenant of Sussex, unveiled the memorial to the officers and men of the 2nd Battalion Royal Sussex Regiment who fell in various campaigns between 1882 - 1902. Those present included the Duke of Devonshire, who was Mayor of Eastbourne, Colonel W. F. Cavaye, Aldermen in their robes and cocked hats, the Town Clerk in wig and gown, Rev. Canon Goodwin, other dignitaries and vast crowds. The monument, sculpted by Mr. Goscombe John, stands on the sea-front between Cavendish Place and the entrance to the pier.

Rough Sea Splash Point, Eastbourne,

THE QUEEN'S HOTEL, p.u. 1909

The Queen's Hotel was designed by Henry Currey and opened in June 1880. It was deliberately planned as a barrier dividing the high-class hotels to the west from the boarding houses to the east. In 1722, foundations of a Roman villa were found on its site and during the construction of the hotel further discoveries were made. The old Eastern Bandstand can be seen on the extreme right of the picture, in the background.

ROUND HOUSE, SPLASH POINT,
EASTBOURNE. 1840.

THE ROUND HOUSE, p.u. 1907
A circular building known as the Round House stood near where the Queen's Hotel stands today.
It was originally built as a windmill in c. 1760, but it was later converted into a marine residence.
The foundations to the Round House were undermined by the sea, and the building was demolished
in 1841.

THE FIELD HOUSE, SPLASH POINT, c. 1869

The Field House was a ten-roomed building which was owned at one time by the Willards, a well-known local family. It was sited near the pier and close to where the famous Carpet Gardens are today, in front of the Burlington Hotel.

45 EASTBOURNE. — *Albion Hotel.* — LL.

THE ALBION HOTEL, p.u. 1906

This was formerly the residence of Lord Ashburnham. Although part of the building dates from 1821, the distinctive tower was not added until 1897. It is reputed to be the first hotel in the town to have had electricity and to be supplied with a telephone (Telephone: Eastbourne 1). Next door is the Albermarle Hotel, originally the Anchor Inn. The 'Anchor' was one of the very early public houses in Eastbourne and an anchor is still visible in the plasterwork on the exterior of the building just below the roof. Also, just visible beyond the Albermarle on the left, are all that remains of Sea Houses, one of which was where Charles Darwin stayed while working on the "Origin of the Species" in the 1850s.

13 EASTBOURNE. — Royal Parade and Band Stand. — LL.

EASTERN BANDSTAND, ROYAL PARADE, c. 1906

In 1894, the Corporation erected the Eastern Bandstand on the beach. But, in 1922, it was moved to the Redoubt Gardens where there was more room and greater access for Bath chairs and perambulators. Some of the original concrete plinths on the beach were used to support a shelter. The Royal Parade was opened by The Prince of Wales, later Edward VII, in 1882. It ends with the great Redoubt, a circular fort built by the government in 1806 during the Napoleonic wars.

THE YORK HOUSE HOTEL, ROYAL PARADE, 1912
York House, built in the late 18th century, has been owned by the Williamson family since 1896.
The hotel has 103 bedrooms, many of which overlook the sea. In the photograph, guests pose
outside the front of the hotel. The photograph was taken by Mr. Geo. Austin, and copies were
available from 70, Seaside.

THE SAN REMO, ROYAL PARADE, c. 1910

The San Remo hotel was built in 1885 and at the turn of the century a warm welcome was assured by Mesdames Dale. In the 1960s the hotel was run by the Martyr family, owners of the Langham Hotel. Today the San Remo is again under independent management.

ROYAL PARADE & REDOUBT. EASTBOURNE.

ROYAL PARADE AND THE REDOUBT, p.u. 1910

On the left is the Langham Hotel, built in 1885 and owned by the same family since 1913, when it was run by the great-grandmother of Mr. Martyr, the present proprietor. Notice the small boys in the sailor suits, one on horseback, passing the hotel. In the background is the Redoubt Fortress, built as part of the defences against Napoleon's threatened invasion. On the right, a horse-drawn 'bus makes its way towards Marine Parade and the Pier.

Royal Parade from Redoubt, Eastbourne

ROYAL PARADE, c. 1910

This part of the Royal Parade looks very similar today with its many small hotels and guest houses. The junction with Addingham Road can be seen on the left.

THE BOWLING GREEN, REDOUBT GARDENS, c. 1910
Another view which has changed very little, especially if you stand with your back to the Redoubt
Fortress and look eastward towards Sovereign Sailing Club and the Lifeboat Station. Bowls can
still be played here but not croquet.

THE SHELTER, REDOUBT, c. 1912

The shelter no longer exists. Behind it in the left background is the Redoubt fortress, which is now a museum and a popular tourist attraction. The mast and coastguard hut have long since disappeared, although the base of the mast still remains.

THE EASTBOURNE COASTGUARD WITH HIS DOG, c. 1905

The coastguard services were set up in Eastbourne in 1822. In 1831 it was reported that the coastguard system was operating and smuggling was declining.

THOMAS HANCOCK, c. 1905

Mr. Thomas Hancock is pictured (right) with his trainer, Mr. (Dippy) Diplock (left) and a large number of cups and trophies. Mr. Hancock, a member of the Eastbourne Swimming Club, was described as the 'champion swimmer of the south coast'. This could well have been so as he was the Sussex County 120 yards Men's Freestyle Champion in 1898 and Sussex County 240 yards Men's Freestyle Champion in 1905 and also in the Eastbourne S.C. water-polo team. Mr. Hancock married and had a son and three daughters. He died in 1941, aged 64 years.

The Duke's Drive, Eastbourne.

UPPER DUKE'S DRIVE, c. 1905

A view that has changed beyond all recognition. The winding road is not visible from this point as the hillside is heavily wooded with ash and sycamore. The Wellcombe Allotments are now on the left, inside the first bend. The area in the right foreground is built up and includes Edensor Road, Coombe Lane and Rowsley Road. Baslow Road joins Duke's Drive from the right. The roads are named after villages in Derbyshire all near to Chatsworth, the home of the Duke of Devonshire.

THE WELLCOMBE, MEADS, EASTBOURNE

THE WELLCOMBE, c. 1925

The Wellcombe is situated in a three-sided hollow in the scarp slope of chalk downland. In the early 19th century, it was part of Colstocks Farm, which was sold in 1865 and is now the site of St. Andrew's Preparatory School (see page 56). The Meads C.E. Primary School can be seen on the left. The houses in Upper Duke's Drive, Edensor, Rowsley and Baslow Roads fill the centre of the picture, with Queenwood Girls' School occupying the high ground just right of centre.

Upper Dukes Drive, Eastbourne. 791

UPPER DUKE'S DRIVE, p.u. 1914
Looking up Upper Duke's Drive, very little has changed except that the trees by the road have grown much larger and there is now a hedge in front of the houses. Twelve semi-detached dwellings, built at the turn of the century, are seen in the foreground. Number 1 is on the left and 12, with its conservatory, on the right. On the extreme right, are numbers 11 and 12 Edensor Road.

"Queenwood," Eastbourne.

QUEENWOOD FROM EDENSOR ROAD, p.u. 1929

Queenwood was formerly a girls' boarding school. In more recent years, it was part of Eastbourne Training College and is now part of Brighton Polytechnic. Perched on the edge of the Wellcombe, it overlooks the old Colstocks Farm area, now St. Andrew's Preparatory School. Girls from Queenwood are seen in the foreground playing lacrosse. The field is now used as a playing area for the Meads C.E. Primary School.

ST. ANDREW'S PREPARATORY SCHOOL, p.u. 1937

St. Andrew's School, founded in 1877, is situated in Meads at the crossroads of Darley Road and Meads Street. Early parish records as far back as 1296, show that the school stands on the site of Colstocks or Wellcombe Farm. Some of the original farm buildings still exist. Many of the houses in Meads Street and in Darley Road have been painted out in the photograph, presumably to show the school in a sylvan setting. There are now no trees across the centre of the school playing fields. St. Andrew's is a co-educational preparatory school with over 400 boarding and day children.

ALDRO SCHOOL, EASTBOURNE. THE HOUSE FROM THE LAWN.

ALDRO SCHOOL, DARLEY ROAD, p.u. 1921

Aldro School was founded in 1898 by the Revd. Harold Browne, brother of the Revd. Edwin Leece Brown, Headmaster of St. Andrew's, Eastbourne (1890 - 1933). During the War, the school was evacuated to Shackleford, near Godalming where it still flourishes. On 16th August 1940, a Messerschmitt ME110 crashed in the grounds of the Aldro. The dead pilot fell onto the roof of the nearby Hill Brow Preparatory School in Bolsover Road and the rear-gunner drowned when he parachuted into the sea. Aldro in Darley Road is now part of Brighton Polytechnic.

MEADS STREET, c. 1910

Photographed at the junction of Darley Road and Meads Street, the view has not altered greatly. The 'bus in the centre of the picture was used in the World's Oldest Municipal Omnibus Service inaugurated on 12th April 1903 between Eastbourne Railway Station and Meads. Notice the advertisement for Coleman's Mustard and the open staircase at the rear of the 'bus. In the background, on the right, is the Ship Hotel and Meads Garage. An advertisement on the wall of the Ship Hotel reads: J. W. Harvey, Electrician.

MEADS STREET, p.u. 1906

Looking south down Meads Street, the view is similar today. There is a plaque on the house on the extreme left which states that it was built in 1897 on the site of the old Ship Inn, which was built in about 1600 (The Ship Inn is now a few metres further down the road on the left-hand side). Derwent Road leads off to the left and the Downs are visible in the background. The four shops with flats above, numbers 48, 50, 52 and 54, are still to be seen on the right.

The shop on the extreme right is the site of the old fire station and dates back to 1898.

MEADS VILLAGE, c. 1910
The small square of houses are architecturally different from the greater part of the area. They
were built by G. A. Wallis for the working class and were known as "Wallis's Cottages". It was
an unusual idea to put all the gardens in the middle of the square.

THE LINKS, MEADS ROAD, p.u. 1920

The Links was built in 1869 and is a particularly good example of the use of local flint as a stone for building. It is situated in Meads Road, almost opposite St. John's Parish Hall by the entrance to Meads Street. The Links was formerly a girls' boarding school specialising in domestic science. It is now used for Methodist Guild holidays.

ST. JOHN'S CHURCH, p.u. 1904

The church was erected in 1869, but destroyed in an air raid in 1942; another victim of fighter bombing. The church tower survived, and later, in 1957, the nave and chancel were rebuilt and St. John's is once again the parish church of Meads.

MOIRA HOUSE SCHOOL, CARLISLE ROAD, p.u. 1914
Moira House was founded in Croydon in 1875 by an enlightened Victorian engineer, who wished girls to have a wide-ranging education, particularly in science. In 1887, the school moved to Eastbourne, where it has remained, except for the war years when it was evacuated to Windermere in the Lake District. Moira House has now just under 400 girls both boarding and day.

80   EASTBOURNE. — View from Paradise. — LL.

THE VIEW FROM PARADISE, p.u. 1905

The view is now much more restricted as trees have grown up on both sides of the road. On the left, in the foreground, is one of the fairways of the Royal Eastbourne Golf Club, which was opened in 1887. In the background, on the left, is the Town Hall and behind it the sea and some of the sea-front hotels.

PARADISE DRIVE, c. 1906

As a result of the hurricane in October 1987, much of the wood was destroyed. Although the Corporation have replanted many trees, it will be years before the wood is restored to its former glory. Just appearing on the left-hand edge of the card is a tiny flint folly which was built on the Compton Estate in 1739. Below the trees on the left is the Royal Eastbourne Golf Course.

SUMMERDOWN CAMP, EASTBOURNE. I.

SUMMERDOWN MILITARY CONVALESCENT CAMP, c. 1916

The Summerdown Military Convalescent Camp was opened during the Great War, as a military convalescent hospital (1915-1920). It is now the site of expensive modern housing in Compton Drive and Old Compton Road. Beyond the camp is Beresford House which is a private girls' school.

The Camp Theatre

Birds Eye View from Downs

Orderly Room & Guard Room

1915 1920

Interior of Ward

The Mascot

Sick Lines

Souvenir
of
Summerdown
Convalescent Camp
— Eastbourne —

Knuts Kamp Komedy Kompany

Blue Boys Band

SUMMERDOWN MILITARY CONVALESCENT CAMP, c. 1920
The souvenir postcard of Summerdown Camp gives some idea of the range of activities available
to the residents. The "Blue Boy's" uniform became a familiar site around Eastbourne.

SUMMERDOWN MILITARY CONVALESCENT CAMP, p.u. 1916
The "Blue Boys", as the soldiers from the military convalescent camp were known, are seen in
one of their sleeping huts - hardly luxurious accommodation even in those days.

ST. CYPRIAN'S, SUMMERDOWN ROAD, p.u. 1913

St. Cyprian's, a boys' preparatory school, moved in 1906 from Carlisle Road to Summerdown Road. The school was run by Mr. L. C. Vaughan Wilkes and Mr. W. J. T. Tomlinson. The children are seen during their corps inspection. It seems that even the very young were preparing for war! The school burned down during the night of Sunday, 14th May 1939. The seventy boys in the school were all saved, but a young maid, 16-year-old Winifred Higgs was a victim of the fire. The boys finished the summer term at Ascham St. Vincent's Preparatory School, but St. Cyprian's moved out of Eastbourne in September 1939 and has since closed. The school grounds are now the site of Eastbourne College Memorial Playing Field.

Ascham St. Vincents, Meads, Eastbourne

ASCHAM ST. VINCENTS, MEADS, c. 1920

Ascham Preparatory School was founded in 1889 by the Revd. William Willis. In 1894, as numbers increased, the school moved to St. Anne's Road. A few years later, the school moved again and this time combined with another preparatory school, St. Vincent's in Carlisle Road, Meads. In 1927, Capt. Arthur Willis took over as Headmaster from his father. In 1938, the school moved to Hazelhurst, but closed two years later. At the end of the war, Eastbourne College purchased the Carlisle Road property and started its own preparatory school. They retained the name Ascham until the school amalgamated with St. Andrew's Preparatory School in 1977. The triangle of land between Carlisle Road, Meads Road amd Gandick Road was sold for housing and all that remains is the Ascham Arch - a war memorial to the forty-nine old boys killed in the 1914-18 War.

Eastbourne   Meads Road.

MEADS ROAD, p.u. 1904

Meads Road joined Meads to the Southbourne area of the town. In the early 19th century,
Eastbourne centred around what is today called the Old Town, with three outlying hamlets called
Meads, Southbourne and Sea Houses.

EASTBOURNE COLLEGE, p.u. 1905

Eastbourne College was founded in 1867 in Spencer Road and opened with just 15 boys under the Headmaster, Dr. Charles Hayman. The foundation stone of the "New Buildings" was laid by Lady Cavendish on 30th July 1870 and this section of the building was completed in 1877. The College Chapel was consecrated in 1874 by the Bishop of Chichester. The College is now a successful public school with about 600 pupils including 60 girls in the 6th form.

" Clovelly," Blackwater Road, Eastbourne.

F. A. Bourne, Photo.

"CLOVELLY", BLACKWATER ROAD

"Clovelly" is in Blackwater Road opposite Eastbourne College. With its flint and brick elevation, it is another fine example of the use of local building materials. "Clovelly" is now divided into flats - such is the fate of many of the fine old houses in Eastbourne. The summer-house on the right of the picture has been removed.

73

Devonshire Park, Eastbourne.

VIEW ACROSS DEVONSHIRE PARK, p.u. 1920

The Devonshire Park was opened by the 7th Duke of Devonshire on 1st July 1874. At one time it was considered as a replacement for the old sports ground that had disappeared with the development of the railway station and Terminus Road area. It was similar to the pavilion and gardens at Buxton, Derbyshire built at the 7th Duke's instigation in 1871. The creation of the Devonshire Park did much to give Eastbourne the name "Empress of Watering Places". The first South of England Grass Tennis Championships were held in 1881 and the Devonshire Park is still one of the leading tennis centres in Britain, hosting many important tennis tournaments. Much of this view is still visible today. The Congress Theatre now partially obstructs the Winter Garden (behind the three trees). Behind the croquet players is the Devonshire Park Theatre, and between the trees is the tower of the old Devonshire Baths.

THE WINTER GARDEN, DEVONSHIRE PARK, p.u. 1906

This was originally referred to as "a miniature Crystal Palace". Much has changed. Most of the glass in the roof has been replaced and the hall is much darker. No longer do palm trees and other exotic plants grow inside the building. The Winter Garden is on two levels. The Floral Hall, as seen in the postcard, was opened first. Soon afterwards, the Pavilion was opened at a higher level. This pavilion, now the Gold Room, was a ballroom and concert hall.

In 1874, the Devonshire Park Orchestra was formed. The first concert, conducted by Julian Adams, took place in July 1876. Eastbourne was the first seaside resort to run a symphony orchestra.

Eastbourne.   Compton Place.   1191

COMPTON PLACE, p.u. 1906

This Jacobean house was built by James Burton and originally called Bourne Place. In 1724, the house was sold to Spencer Compton. Later Compton Place fell into the hands of the Cavendish family in Eastbourne. The house has accommodated many royal and important visitors, including Edward VII, George V, Queen Mary and Queen Elizabeth, as a child. Since 1954, the house has been occupied by the Ladies' School of English.

The hunt featured in the foreground is most likely the East Sussex, founded in 1853. The East Sussex amalgamated with the Romney Marsh in 1966.

THE KING'S VISIT TO EASTBOURNE, JULY 11TH 1903.

Printed in Hessen.

Published by W. Brooker, Station, Eastbourne.

KING EDWARD VII's VISIT TO EASTBOURNE, 1903

King Edward VII visited Eastbourne on Saturday, 11th July 1903. The royal train arrived at Eastbourne Station just before 5 p.m. and the King was welcomed by the Duke of Devonshire, the Mayor and Corporation. Following a loyal address from the Mayor, Cllr. Dr. O'Brien Harding, the King inspected cadets from Eastbourne College. He was then conveyed by carriage and horses to Compton Place, where he stayed as a guest of the Duke and Duchess of Devonshire. The postcard shows the King, escorted by two outriders and four mounted police, on his extended route taken to Compton Place via Terminus Road, Cornfield Road, Devonshire Place, Grand Parade, Carlisle Road, College Road, Blackwater Road, Grange Road, Meads Road and Compton Place Road. The next day the King attended Divine Service at St. Peter's Church and then paid a surprise visit to the Princess Alice Memorial Hospital.

THE SAFFRONS CRICKET GROUND, p.u. 1910

The Saffrons, Compton Place Road, was opened in 1886 because the Duke of Devonshire required the old ground for development. There is now a new pavilion and many of the trees have gone. Sussex County Cricket Club still have an annual week in August. The Saffrons is the home of Eastbourne Cricket Club, Eastbourne Town Football Club, Eastbourne Hockey Club and other local sporting organisations.

SAFFRONS ROAD, p.u. 1908
Saffrons Road, which runs on the north-east side of the Saffrons Cricket and Football ground,
remains much the same today, apart from the motor-cars parked along the street!

THE TOWN HALL, c. 1910

In 1851, the Vestry Room (forerunner of the present Town Hall) was built in Grove Road. In 1874, the Local Board (forerunner to the Town Council) proposed the building of a new Town Hall. The building was designed in Renaissance style by W. T. Foulkes of Birmingham, with the foundation stone laid by Lord Edward Cavendish on 9th October 1884. It was built in dark red brick, dressed with Portland stone, on the site of the old Stocks Bank, previously the site of the St. George's Day Fair (12th March) which was held up to the beginning of the 19th century. The Town Hall was completed in 1886 at a cost of £40,000. It was opened by the Mayor, George Boulton in 1886 to the accompaniment of Handel's Hallelujah Chorus, Haydn's The Heavens are Telling, and the National Anthem. The 130 ft.-high clock tower contains a one ton bell and four smaller bells. When it first opened, the Town Hall accommodated the Corporation Offices, the police and the County Courts.

PROCLAMATION OF KING GEORGE V, 1910

The postcard shows the Duke of Devonshire, then Mayor of Eastbourne, reading the proclamation of King George V from the balcony of the Town Hall at midday on Monday, 9th May 1910 in front of a crowd of several thousand people. At the front of the crowd can be seen the Eastbourne College Cadets (OTC) in khaki and a number of Scouts. Immediately 12 o'clock struck, the Eastbourne Municipal Orchestra under Mr. Hiram Henton struck up a fanfare. The orchestra was situated in front of the crowd.

SOUTH STREET, c. 1870

South Street was part of the old hamlet of Southbourne. The old houses on the left, in the foreground, are still there today. They are centred around the Dickens Tea Rooms. Stocks Bank would have been behind the artist's viewpoint and the Town Hall had not yet been built. The postcard is one of the series 'Ye old Eastbourne' and based on a watercolour by J. Owen.

SOUTH STREET, c. 1870

This was part of the hamlet of Southbourne as seen from Gildredge Road looking towards what would have been Stocks Bank. Very little of the original housing is left. The Old Eastbourne Theatre has disappeared; it was on the left where Llewellyn's Builders have their offices today. Haine and Sons, funeral directors, are seen on the right and are probably the only original business still operating in South Street. The postcard is based on a watercolour by J. Owen in the same series 'Ye old Eastbourne'.

Orchard Road and Institute, Eastbourne

THE TECHNICAL INSTITUTE AND FREE LIBRARY, p.u. 1906

The first public library was housed in the Vestry Hall in Grove Road in 1896. The 8th Duke of Devonshire donated a site in Grove Road for a new Public Library and Technical Institute in 1899. The Vestry Hall was demolished in 1902 and the foundation stone for the new building was laid on the site by the Duke of Devonshire on 25th April 1903. The new building was designed by P. A. Robson and the building costs totalled £38,000, with a generous £10,000 donation from Mr. Andrew Carnegie and £2,000 from the East Sussex County Council. The Public Library and Technical Institute were officially opened by the Duchess of Devonshire on 8th August 1904. The building also contained the School of Art and a museum which included the "Arnold" collection of 300 stuffed birds. It was destoyed by bombing in February and June 1943. After being housed in temporary accommodation in Grand Parade, the new Public Library in Grove Road opened to the public on 6th April 1964.

THE GILBERT ARMS, c. 1870
On the corner of Grove Road, opposite the station, was Hartfield farmhouse, which was later converted to the Gilbert Arms public house, popularly known as The Squirrel.

Terminus Road & Station, Eastbourne.

THE RAILWAY STATION, p.u. 1905

In 1849 the railway line was extended from Polegate to Eastbourne by the London, Brighton and South Coast Railway. The present station is the fourth on the' site. The land around the station was owned by Charles Gilbert (Lord of Gildredge Manor). The coming of the railway was vital to the plans of the Gilbert and Compton estates for the development of modern Eastbourne.

On the right of the picture, the 'bus, reg. no. AP 295, is ready to depart to Ocklynge Road.

EASTBOURNE RAILWAY STATION, c. 1906

A superb interior view of Eastbourne Station. Above the bookstall a wealth of detail can be seen. The advertisements include: Shelvey's Aerated Waters; Stephen's ink; Hall's tonic; Shelvey's ginger beer; and Davison & Co., Sussex Stores. The bookstall advertises fountain pens at 2/6d (12½p) and various picture books at 6d (2½p) and 1/- (5p).

Eastbourne Station was damaged on many occasions during the War. The area to the north has been developed into a market and enterprise centre.

WATCHING ELECTION RESULTS. EASTBOURNE. FLASHLIGHT PHOTO BY F.C.COOPER. DEC 1910.
AT "GAZETTE" OFFICE.

ELECTION RESULTS AT THE "GAZETTE" OFFICE, 1910
This postcard shows the crowds watching and waiting for the General Election results outside
the Gazette (Newspaper) Office at about 10-30 p.m. on Monday, 12th December 1910. The seat
for Eastbourne was won by Mr. Rupert Gwynne (Conservative and Unionist).

THE EASTBOURNE TOWN CRIER, p.u. 1907

This postcard shows the Eastbourne Town Crier, Mr. Clement Reed. He is most probably standing outside the Cavendish Hotel, Grand Parade, or on the corner of Cornfield Road and Terminus Road, where the Midland Bank now stands. Mr. Reed was born in 1848, married at St. Mary's Church, Old Town on 8th November 1877 and died on 10th January 1906 as a result of a fall from a 'bus in the Goffs. The dog was not his, but used to follow him around and seems to be competing for attention.

Town Crier and Dog, Eastbourne.

1775 Eastbourne Victoria Place

VICTORIA PLACE, p.u. 1914

Victoria Place still exists, but it is now an extension of Terminus Road which ends at the sea-front just west of the Pier by the Burlington Hotel. In the right foreground, the Royal Victoria Sea-Water Baths no longer exist. Notice the splendid old weighing-machine by the entrance to the Baths and the London, Brighton and South Coast Railway horse-drawn delivery wagon.

TERMINUS ROAD, c. 1906

If you stand outside Debenhams today and look back up Terminus Road, it is still possible to see the Downs. In the distance is the distinctive top of the Lewes Old Bank. The shops on view include E. Smith & Son on the left and C. J. Vinall, general draper and house furnisher, on the right. Notice the men carrying sandwich boards in the middle of the road. The advent of the shopping precinct has altered this view considerably.

52 EASTBOURNE. — Lewes old Bank. — LL.

THE LEWES OLD BANK, c. 1906
The Lewes Old Bank was situated at the junction of Terminus Road and Cornfield Road. The original bank was bombed and destroyed by a 500kg. bomb on 7th March 1943, and in its place today stands the Terminus branch of Barclays Bank. The southern end of Junction Road, the small street on the left of the photograph, has disappeared as a result of the building of the Arndale Centre.

119 EASTBOURNE. — Terminus Road. — LL.

TERMINUS ROAD, p.u. 1916

Looking down Terminus Road and photographed at the junctions with Trinity Trees, on the left, and Seaside Road, on the right. Dale and Kerley, drapers and milliners, later became Barker's, and the site is now occupied by the A. & N. department store. John Nix, jeweller and silversmith, is now occupied by a newsagents.

TERMINUS ROAD, c. 1906

Atkinson & Co. occupied the building on the corner of Lismore and Terminus Roads. Later it became Bobby's department store, which was narrowly missed during a bombing raid on 8th October 1940. Bobby's closed in the mid-1970s and the building is now occupied by Debenhams. Notice the ornate gas lamp in the right foreground.

66 EASTBOURNE. — Terminus Road and Gildridge Hotel. — LL.

THE GILDREDGE HOTEL, TERMINUS ROAD, p.u. 1915

The Gildredge Hotel still stands outside the railway station in Terminus Road. It was badly damaged by enemy bombing on Friday, 22nd November 1940. An interesting variety of vehicles are shown on the postcard including an early motor 'bus, a horse-drawn omnibus, and a delivery waggon belonging to Sutton & Co., carriers. The gas lamp in the foreground also doubled as a 'bus stop.

95

Princess Alice Hospital, Eastbourne.

THE PRINCESS ALICE HOSPITAL, CAREW ROAD, p.u. 1910

The Princess Alice Hospital was built in memory of Princess Alice who was the second daughter of Queen Victoria, and who became the Grand Duchess of Hesse. She suffered from ill-health and came to Eastbourne to convalesce, but died in December 1878 aged 35 years. On 30th June 1883, the Prince of Wales opened the hospital, the extended western promenade and the lawns on the sea-front, and the Bedford Well Pumping Station. In addition, he attended lunch at the Winter Garden and tea at Compton Place.

Princess Alice's Tree and South Street, Eastbourne

...or, Stationer, Eastbourne.   a 153|118

PRINCESS ALICE'S TREE AND SMITH STREET, c. 1915

Looking down South Street and photographed from Memorial Square, where the War Memorial stands today. At the time, the central building was occupied by H. R. Bourne, chemist and druggist, and to the right was a grocer's shop. The large tree, on the right, was known as Princess Alice's Tree having been planted by her on one of her visits to Eastbourne. On the left, St. Saviour's Church was designed by G. E. Street. It was built in red brick with the total building costs paid by Mr. G. Whelpton. The church was consecrated in 1872 and following a thanksgiving service, the vicar, the Revd. H. R. Whelpton, climbed the 176 ft.-high spire and set a weathercock atop. The congregation below sang "Pleasant are thy courts above!"

Trinity Trees, Seaside Road, Eastbourne.

TRINITY TREES, p.u. 1904

Looking west along Trinity Trees one can see the spire of St. Saviour's Church and the Downs in the background. Holy Trinity Church, which lies behind the trees on the left, was consecrated in 1839. Trinity Trees used to be part of Seaside Road and joined the hamlets of Southbourne and Sea Houses.

SEASIDE ROAD, c. 1906

Looking in a north-easterly direction along Seaside Road and photographed close to the junction with Queen's Gardens, on the right. The business premises on the left include: a ladies' and gentlemen's hairdressing saloon - 37, Seaside; The Devonshire Hotel owned by the Star Brewery Co., with W. Wells the proprietor at the time; and the Theatre Royal - now the Hippodrome and still a working theatre. On the right, the parade includes a garage, and in the foreground, Hope's clothing store.

Tidal Wave, Seaside, Eastbourne.

TIDAL WAVE, SEASIDE, p.u. 1917
Before the First World War, postcards were used to record events and disasters and these have
now become highly collectable. This card illustrates the flooding of Seaside caused by a freak
tidal wave - the actual date is unknown. Seaside still occasionally suffers flooding from the sea
at various times of the year and is particularly at risk when there are spring tides and a southerly
gale, but due to the sea-wall being strengthened and improved, flooding on this scale has been
curtailed. On the right is the Leaf Hall, with its church-like tower.

THE LEAF HALL, SEASIDE, c. 1906

During the nineteenth century, there was considerable concern for the welfare of the working classes and the social problems caused by alcohol. A Mr. William Leaf decided to donate a generous sum of money towards the building of a recreation centre where men could spend their leisure time in sober pursuits. This resulted in the building of the Leaf Hall which was opened in 1864. The hall is now used as the Eastbourne Karate Centre.

Opposite the Leaf Hall, the Bourne stream ended in a pond known as Broadbourne. The water then seeped through the shingle into the sea.

LEAF HALL.
EASTBOURNE.

MOTCOMBE GARDENS, OLD TOWN, p.u. 1919

Geographically, the settlement around St. Mary's Church, Old Town, is a springline settlement. Motcombe Park, as it is today, was part of Motcombe Farm. The renovated farm house still stands in Motcombe Road opposite the park. The pond in Motcombe Park is the source (spring) of the Bourne stream. The pond used to cover a larger area, but in 1857 it was altered to its present shape. It was the water supply for the town and therefore subject to public health rules until about 1850. The park was given to the Corporation by the Duke of Devonshire in 1910.

GILDREDGE PARK, c. 1910

In 1888, the council leased the land from Carew Davies Gilbert, Lord of the Manor. In 1908, the council purchased the whole area. The Manor House and its gardens are situated in the north-west corner of this beautiful park. The house was purchased for the town in 1922 and opened in 1923 as the Towner Art Gallery. Many trees in the park were uprooted during the hurricane of 1987, but much replanting has been done since.

Old Town, Eastbourne.

HIGH STREET, OLD TOWN, c. 1910

Looking up High Street towards St. Mary's Church and the beginning of Church Street. Many changes have occured to the buildings over the years. In the left foreground, the building is now occupied by an off-licence, and further up the site is now a garage complex. On the right, below the Lamb Inn, the buildings and tree have disappeared to make way for a Safeway's Supermarket.

Out of view, on the left, are the Manor House and gardens, now the Towner Art Gallery.

The Old Parsonage, Eastbourne.

THE OLD PARSONAGE, c. 1906

Originally, the Old Parsonage was built as a Tudor Rectory Manor in the 16th century. The construction of the walls was unusual in that they were made of rubble masonry (sandstone, flint and mortar). By the end of the nineteenth century, the building had fallen into a state of ill-repair. In 1912, the Parsonage was bought by the Duke of Devonshire and presented to the parish, together with a large contribution towards the cost of restoration. The Old Parsonage is to be found next to St. Mary's Church, Old Town, and is now used as the parish hall.

Ocklynge Road, Old Town, Eastbourne.

THE LAMB HOTEL, p.u. 1904

The 14th-century Lamb Hotel is the oldest public house in Eastbourne and was built using local greensand. The postcard shows the unrecognisable exterior of the inn with its walls rendered with plaster. At the time the licensee was W. F. Walton. On the left, the poster on the wall advertises pleasure trips from Eastbourne by the L.B. & S.C. Railway.

THE LAMB INN, OLD TOWN, c. 1920
The Lamb Hotel photographed after the alterations to the building in 1912, when the plaster was removed to reveal the original timbers. Compare the position of the first-floor windows with the postcard on the opposite page. Edward Miller was the proprietor at the time the photograph was taken.

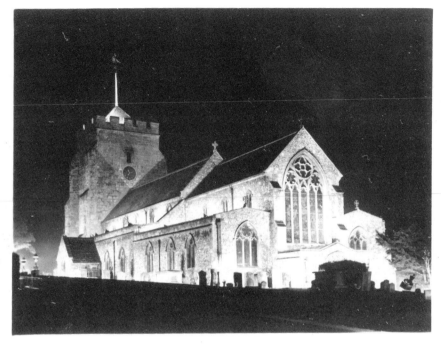

SILVER JUBILEE
MAY 1935

ST. MARY'S
PARISH CHURCH
EASTBOURNE

FLOODLIGHTED
BY
EASTBOURNE
GAS COMPANY

ST. MARY'S CHURCH, OLD TOWN, 1935

St. Mary's Church is dedicated to St. Mary the Virgin. It was erected in the twelfth century to replace a Saxon church dedicated to St. Michael, probably a wooden structure, of which no traces are left. The church is seen floodlit by the Eastbourne Gas Company during celebrations to mark the Silver Jubilee of King George V.

Tally-Ho, Old Town, Eastbourne. 607.

THE TALLY-HO, OLD TOWN, p.u. 1907

The Tally-Ho public house stands on the corner of Church Street, opposite the site of the former St. Mary's Hospital. The Tally-Ho sign depicts a hunting scene. It is probably coincidental that on Boxing Day, 1886, a collier ship called the *Tally-Ho* was driven ashore onto the beach at Eastbourne, while sailing from Sunderland to Littlehampton. St. Mary's Hospital was originally a cavalry barracks during the Napoleonic War and later became a workhouse before becoming a hospital.

THE OLD POST OFFICE, OCKLYNGE ROAD, 1865
Standing outside the Post Office in Ocklynge Road, one looks over houses where these cottages and the old Post Office used to stand just below St. Mary's Church. In 1865 the sub-postmaster was T. Pain.

OCKLYNGE, c. 1910

Photographed at the junction of Upperton Road, Gore Park Avenue and Selwyn Road, and looking north to Willingdon Road. At the time, the parade of shops included (right to left): a chemist; a branch of the International Stores; a butcher; and at the end of the parade, tea rooms. The open-topped omnibus, reg. no. AP 2035, is about to depart from Ocklynge Road to the Railway Station. Notice the solid tyres and the lack of protection for the driver in inclement weather conditions. Behind the driver, a sign reads: 'No smoking allowed'.

Hampden Park, Eastbourne

HAMPDEN PARK, p.u. 1905
Hampden Park was purchased from Lord Willingdon for £3000 and opened to the public in 1901.
The large lake, shown on the postcard, was formerly known as the Decoy Pond. The Park is
a popular area today, with a lake, woods, tennis courts, bowling greens and playing fields.

THE TEA HOUSE, HAMPDEN PARK, c. 1910
Refreshments are still available from the 'Tea House' in Hampden Park.

THE BEACHY HEAD HOTEL, c. 1906

The Beachy Head Hotel was formerly known as the Queen's Hotel. It was destroyed by fire, first in the 1920s and then in 1966. The hotel was rebuilt and a much larger building now stands on the site, providing visitors with excellent views across Bullock Down and towards Belle Tout.

BEACHY HEAD, p.u. 1916

The famous chalk headland lies halfway between Eastbourne and Birling Gap, rising to a height of 534 feet and one of the highest cliffs on the Sussex coastline. The name Beachy Head originates from the Norman-French "Beau-Chef" meaning fair head or promontary. This early comic card shows a fairly accurate outline of the head.

Have just Climbed to the top of BEACHY HEAD!

BEACHY HEAD, c. 1910

The top of Beachy Head has always been a popular beauty spot with holidaymakers and local residents, who are rewarded with spectacular views in all directions. Great care must be taken if walking close to the cliff edge, as the chalk cliffs are soft and dangerous. During the winter months there are frequent cliff falls which have resulted in considerable erosion of both the cliff face and the land on the top of Beachy Head.

BEACHY HEAD LIGHTHOUSE, p.u. 1906

In 1899, Trinity House decided that a new lighthouse should be built at the base of Beachy Head, to replace Belle Tout lighthouse which had been built on the cliffs above. Belle Tout was under serious threat from cliff erosion, and the light was frequently obscured by sea mists which provided a serious risk to seafarers. A survey of the seabed revealed a suitable site for the foundations about 500 ft. from the base of the cliffs. A coffer-dam was constructed on the site, and after high water, the water was pumped out to allow work to continue. A platform similar to a small oil-rig was erected alongside, and from the top of the cliffs a cableway, with a span of over 600 ft., ran down to the platform. The cables (one of which was 6″ in diameter with a breaking strain of 120 tons) carried the dressed stones and building materials to the tower. Over 3,600 tons of Cornish granite were used and the lighthouse was completed in February 1902. The lighthouse is 142 ft. high, with the light having a range of 25 miles. In 1983, it was made fully automatic and is now unmanned.

The lighthouse featured on the 22 pence postage stamp for the 'Safety at Sea' issue on 18th June 1985,

S.S. EASTFIELD STRANDED AT BEACHY HEAD DEC /09.   F.C.C.

THE S.S. EASTFIELD STRANDED AT BEACHY HEAD, c. 1909

At about 3 a.m. on Friday, 3rd December 1909, the S.S. *Eastfield* (2,355 tons) was driven ashore in a gale, 200 metres east of the disused Belle Tout lighthouse. The *Eastfield* was on her way, in ballast, from Hull to Barry in South Wales. The ship, under the command of Captain Barrington had a crew of 21, including a stowaway who "was set to work after his presence on board was discovered". The captain did not launch the ship's lifeboat, which was fortunate, as at low water the crew were able to walk round to Birling Gap and safety. On Sunday, 5th December, hundreds of people from Eastbourne, Seaford and the neighbouring villages visited the wreck.

OLD (BELLE TOUT) LIGHTHOUSE, BEACHY HEAD

BELLE TOUT LIGHTHOUSE, c. 1900

In the early 18th century, the Reverend Jonathan Darby, rector of Litlington and vicar of East Dean and Friston, provided his own aid for sailors. On rough stormy nights, Parson Darby hung lights in the caves below the cliff to guide shipwrecked sailors to safety. One of these caves was known as "Darby's Hole". The Reverend Darby eventually fell victim to his own philanthropy, dying of pneumonia in 1728. The inscription on his gravestone in East Dean Churchyard reads "he was a friend to sailors". Darby's Hole has long disappeared. By 1828 a small hut housing a light was placed at the top of the cliffs at Belle Tout. This was replaced in 1834 by a 47ft.-high circular stone tower built by John Fuller, M.P. The light remained in operation until 1902 when it was replaced by the new Beachy Head lighthouse. Belle Tout, named after an Iron Age fort, is situated about one mile west of Beachy Head.

Oxen on Downs, near Eastbourne

OXEN ON THE DOWNS NEAR EASTBOURNE, p.u. 1919
The last pair of working oxen were on the Downs at Birling Manor c. 1925. Oxen were slow-moving animals and remote barns on the Downs were used to shelter these animals rather than bring them back to the main farmyard overnight and drive them out again next day.